Lost and Found
A Story About Honesty

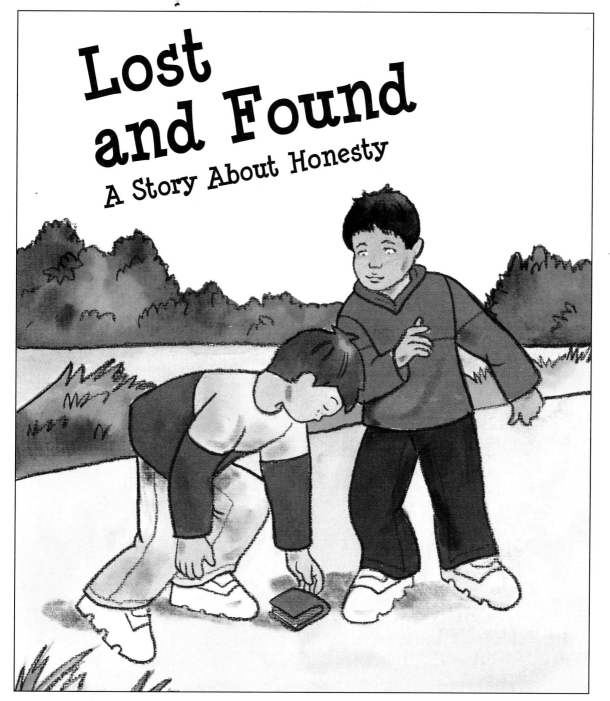

Written by
Cindy Leaney

Illustrated by
Peter Wilks

Rourke
Publishing LLC
Vero Beach, Florida 32964

Before you read this story, take a look at the front cover of the book. Try to guess what Matt and José have found on the road.

1. What are they going to do with what they've found?

2. And what could they do that would be honest?

Produced by SGA Illustration and Design
Designed by Phil Kay
Series Editor: Frank Sloan

www.rourkepublishing.com

Library of Congress Cataloging-in-Publication Data

Leaney, Cindy.
    Lost and Found : honesty / by Cindy Leaney ; illustrated by Peter Wilks.
        p. cm. -- (Hero club character)
    Summary: Matt and José decide to take the wallet they find on the street to the police station even though they need extra money to go to the fair.
    ISBN 1-58952-736-4
    [1. Honesty--Fiction. 2. Conduct of life--Fiction.] I. Wilks, Peter, ill. II. Title.

PZ7.L46335Lq2003
[E]--dc21
                                                                            2003043233

Printed in the USA
MP/W

Welcome to The Hero Club!
Read about all the things that happen to them.
Try and guess what they'll do next.

www.theheroclub.com

"How much more do we need, Matt?"

"Five dollars."

"Let's go over to my house and ask Mom if she wants the car washed."

"Wow. Look at this, José.
Somebody dropped a wallet."

"Whose is it?"

"I don't know.
There's nothing in here
but lots of money."

"What should we do?"

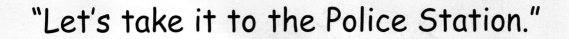

"Let's take it to the Police Station."

"We could just take five dollars
out first.
There's over a hundred here.
They probably wouldn't mind.
They might not even notice."

"What if they did?"

"What if they've been saving for something? How would you feel if that was your dad's wallet?"

"Yeah, you're right.
Let's walk over there.
It's just a few blocks."

"Hi, kids. What can I do for you?"

"We found this wallet.
There's nothing in it to say who
it belongs to."

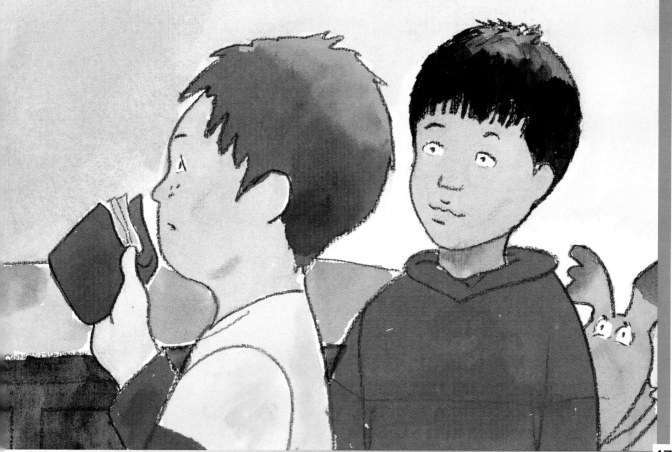

"Somebody called and reported it lost about an hour ago. The owner just moved here. You did the right thing."

"No, I guess not."

"Kids! There's somebody here to see you."

"No, that's okay."

WHAT DO YOU THINK?

Was it a good idea for Matt and José to take the wallet to the Police Station?

Why or why not?

IMPORTANT IDEAS

Honest—a person who is honest does not lie, cheat, or steal.

On page 19, the police officer says, "You did the right thing."

The opposite of honest is dishonest.

Have you ever found something valuable? What would you do if you did?

Now that you have read this book, see if you can answer these questions:

1. What do Matt and José find in the road and what is inside it?

2. Is there anybody's name in the wallet? Does this make it harder for the boys to know what to do?

3. What does the man offer Matt and José as a reward?

About the author

Cindy Leaney teaches English and writes books for both young readers and adults. She has lived and worked in England, Kenya, Mexico, Saudi Arabia, and the United States.

About the illustrator

Peter Wilks began work in advertising, where he developed a love for illustration. He has drawn pictures for many children's books in Great Britain and in the United States.

HERO CLUB CHARACTER VALUE SERIES

Everyone Makes a Difference (A Book About Community)

Field Trip (A Book About Sharing)

It's Your Turn Now (A Book About Politeness)

Lost and Found (A Book About Honesty)

Summer Vacation (A Book About Patience)

Taking Care of Mango (A Book About Responsibility)